Praise for *The Kingdom Assignment*

What an incredible example of the Prayer of Jabez is occurring in the lives of Denny and Leesa Bellesi and Coast Hills Community Church! Don't miss this amazing story of one couple and one church who actually put the prayer "Please enlarge our borders" into practice in a bold and revolutionary manner. Don't miss this miracle!

— BRUCE WILKINSON
AUTHOR OF *THE PRAYER OF JABEZ*

What Denny and Leesa experienced with the Kingdom Assignment was inarguably a "God Thing" . . . unexpected, supernatural, and transforming!

— BILL HYBELS
SENIOR PASTOR OF WILLOW CREEK COMMUNITY CHURCH

There is something amazingly energizing and rewarding when we fulfill the purpose for which we are created . . . reflecting the goodness of God through our good works. The stories in this book are the dramatic evidence. Buy a case of these books for your friends!

— PAUL ESHELMAN
DIRECTOR/THE *JESUS* FILM PROJECT
VICE PRESIDENT/CAMPUS CRUSADE FOR CHRIST

The Bellesis have written of miracle after miracle that have come about as part of the Kingdom Assignment. I could not stop reading until I had read every act of God's grace and the faithfulness by His people.

— STEPHEN ARTERBURN
FOUNDER, WOMEN OF FAITH

I love this book! This inspiring Kingdom adventure will have you cheering, wiping away tears, and unabashedly celebrating what God can do through a few people who gain a vision for impacting a community.

— LEE STROBEL
AUTHOR, *THE CASE FOR CHRIST* AND *THE CASE FOR FAITH*

This is one of the most inspiring stories I've ever heard from a church in America. The Kingdom Assignment *encouraged my family and myself to take on the same challenge Denny and Leesa Bellesi handed out to their congregation. What a responsibility and a life-changing blessing!*

— JIM BURNS, PH.D.
PRESIDENT, YOUTHBUILDERS

. . . this book, The Kingdom Assignment, *can revolutionize your life and your church.*

— RICK WARREN
LEAD PASTOR, SADDLEBACK CHURCH
AUTHOR, *THE PURPOSE-DRIVEN® CHURCH*

The Kingdom Assignment *is motivating proof that "giving" generously, outrageously, spontaneously, and radically is the key to living life to its fullest. It will change your life, your community, and the world around you!*

— BECKY TIRABASSI
AUTHOR, *CHANGE YOUR LIFE*
GUEST CONTRIBUTOR *THE CBS EARLY SHOW*

THE KINGDOM ASSIGNMENT

THE KINGDOM ASSIGNMENT

WHAT WILL YOU DO WITH
THE TALENTS GOD HAS GIVEN YOU?

• DENNY AND LEESA BELLESI •

GRAND RAPIDS, MICHIGAN 49530

ZONDERVAN™

The Kingdom Assignment
Copyright © 2001 by Denny Bellesi and Leesa Bellesi

Requests for information should be addressed to:

Zondervan, *Grand Rapids, Michigan 49530*

Library of Congress Cataloging-in-Publication Data

Bellesi, Denny, 1951–.
    The kingdom assignment : what will you do with the talents God has
given you? / Denny and Leesa Bellesi.
        p. cm.
    ISBN 0-310-24323-8
    1. Stewardship, Christian.   2. Coast Hills Community Church
(Aliso Viejo, Calif.)—Charities.   I. Bellesi, Leesa, 1955–.   II. Title.
BV772.b B47 2001
248'.6—dc21

2001026970

This edition printed on acid-free paper.

Published in association with the literary agency of Alive Communications,
Inc., 7680 Goddard Street, Suite 200, Colorado Springs, CO 80920.

Interior design by Beth Shagene

Printed in the United States of America

---

01 02 03 04 05 06 07 08 /❖ DC/ 10 9 8 7 6 5 4 3 2

*This book is dedicated
to the thousands of people
who have helped make
Coast Hills Community Church
and this marked event
called the Kingdom Assignment
a reality.
Thank you for holding the bar
of excellence high in our pursuit
to extend the Kingdom of Jesus Christ
across every boundary
to every generation.*

Contents

Acknowledgments

It has been by God's grace that we stand before you as partners, writing with one mind, one heart, and one purpose. We thank God for his faithfulness and for the efforts of Ginny Leck, Greg Johnson at Alive Communications, Karen Kingsbury, John Sloan, and the entire staff at Zondervan, all of whom have made this Kingdom Assignment a pure joy in our lives.

An Assignment
That Changed Their Lives

♕♕♕♕♕♕♕♕♕♕♕♕♕♕♕♕♕

I have an assignment for you that will change your life.

A Kingdom Assignment.

Before you say no, before you tell me you're too busy, too untrained, or too ill-equipped to handle one more assignment—especially one for the Kingdom of God—think about this:

If you accept the assignment, you will take a small amount of money and increase it up to a hundredfold or more. You will have the means to help countless people—some with food and clothing, others with medicine or the gospel message—and in the process, no matter how much money your investment turns into, no matter how many people you will help, you will walk away with more than what your investment will ever make and more than those you've invested in.

Interested?

♕♕♕♕♕♕♕♕♕♕♕♕♕♕♕♕♕

That was the proposal I gave to one hundred people at the church I pastor in Southern California. Each person was given $100 on three conditions. First, that they understand the money belongs to God; second, that they invest it in God's work; and third, that they report the results in ninety days.

The reports came in on February 7, 2001, to an overflow crowd of nearly two thousand people crammed into our church building. The facts were unbelievable. In just three months $10,000 had become more than $100,000. Thousands of people had been clothed or fed or brought into a relationship with God. Whole communities were changed in the process, and now, everyone wanted to know about the Kingdom Assignment.

There were cars parked half a mile away as people streamed through the doors. The buzz in the room was the type usually reserved for rock concerts, not Wednesday night worship services.

All one hundred participants had invited guests—in some cases entire neighborhoods—each one with a story to tell. Tissues were passed out at the door, and NBC's *Dateline* was on hand to capture the event for national television.

Then one by one the stories came.

People spoke in tears about how the Kingdom Assignment had given them an entirely different approach to life. There were stories of how a $100 bill became $13,000 and how whole churches were started up with that simple, small amount. My wife, Leesa, showed a videotape she'd made detailing the stories from dozens of others. Tears flowed throughout the night and no one was left untouched.

The results of the Kingdom Assignment were beyond anything Leesa or I ever dared to dream. And we'd been dreaming of this assignment for many, many years.

Like many of you, I was raised in the church and grew up believing the Christian faith was only about getting to heaven. As an active child, I had no interest in death and dying, let alone heaven. I pictured clouds, harps, angels, that kind of thing, and believed it held no relevance whatsoever to my life.

No surprise that church attendance was not a priority for me back then. It was boring and irrelevant. As a young teenager, I remember waking up early on Sunday mornings and doing all I could to keep my sisters quiet and the television sound turned down low. I even tried setting all the clocks back in hopes my parents would oversleep and forget about the whole thing.

Heaven could wait, as far as I was concerned. There were many more important things to do. It wasn't until my high school years that Jesus Christ had any real impact on my life. Even then, heaven wasn't the driving motivation. Heaven was just the frosting on the cake.

What captivated me was the everyday practicality of trying to live like Jesus.

I began noticing how often the Kingdom was mentioned in the Gospels. How people related and worked and played and loved one another in the Kingdom. And eventually I began to realize that the Kingdom Jesus was referring to wasn't some faraway heavenly place.

It was right here, right now.

Suddenly, everything became clear. Being a Christian wasn't about getting to heaven, although that was a benefit. It was about becoming part of the Kingdom among us, the one that is far too easy to miss unless we're looking. I understood for the first time that the Kingdom of God wasn't a place in the clouds or a dot on a map, but a reality that begins deep within us as we give our lives over to Jesus.

The truth that hit home hardest was this: The benefits of Kingdom living can be realized now, without another moment's hesitation.

This book is about a hundred people who decided to take Jesus at His Word. It's the story of how they volunteered to take on a Kingdom Assignment, in which they were commissioned to think and act like Kingdom people. And it's the story of how that assignment changed their lives and the lives of countless others around them.

And if you accept the assignment? It will change your life forever—and the lives of countless others around you for today, tomorrow, and all eternity.

Set aside the next hour and imagine you were in church the day the Kingdom Assignment was given. Sit in the room as the excitement around these hundred people first began to grow and then explode in their individual worlds.

Throughout the journey of these next few chapters, consider this: At the end of this book you'll be asked to take on a Kingdom Assignment of your own. If you accept ... be ready. Because you'll never, ever be the same again.

—DENNY AND LEESA BELLESI

An initial manifestation of God's Kingdom is found in the mission of our Lord on earth. . . . We may therefore now experience its power; we may know its life; we may enter into a participation of its blessings. If we have entered into the enjoyment of the blessings of God's Kingdom, our final question is: What are we to do as a result of these blessings?

—GEORGE ELDON LADD

CHAPTER 1

"I Need 100 Volunteers . . ."

With $10,000 wadded up in my pocket, I was about to do what I'd never heard of any other pastor doing: Walk down the aisle and start handing out $100 bills. My heart raced and my hands sweated. After decades of dreaming, it had finally come down to this.

The idea had been lurking in the shadows of my mind since my youth worker days, but always the problem was the same: If we are going to give a hundred people a hundred dollars, where do we get the money?

It's Time!

The answer came in a darkened theater halfway through the movie *Pay It Forward*. Starring Kevin

Spacey, Helen Hunt, and Haley Joel Osment, it's the story about a young boy who is challenged by his junior high school teacher to come up with an idea that could "change the world," and then dare to put it into action.

The movie triggered an idea that hit Leesa and me almost at the same time. We simply looked at each other and said, "It's time!" Oblivious to the others in the theater trying to enjoy the movie, we put the popcorn between us and munched away, talking nonstop about how this would come together. Our excitement quickly traveled from our hearts to our voices. All at once we heard three loud "Shhhh's!" We slumped a little farther down in our seats and tried to keep quiet through the rest of the movie.

As soon as the credits rolled, I reminded her of my series of sermons that I had coming up and that it seemed like a perfect time to play out our dream of the parable of the talents with our very own congregation. Leesa's expression changed and her eyes began a wondrous dance of anticipation. "Okay," she swallowed hard. "But where will you get the money?"

It was a question I took to our Missions Outreach Team that week. I explained that there were more than enough funds in the church account earmarked for local outreach.

A hush fell over the room.

"You want to give $100 to a hundred people and ask them to invest it for God?" one member asked.

I nodded. "Dream with me here," I told them. "We're not talking about a means to an end. We're talking about an explosion of Kingdom participants acting on behalf of the King. It's the kind of project that could change the world."

"Ten thousand dollars?" The question was little more than a whisper.

I blinked, then made eye contact with every team member. "Something tells me this is what Jesus would do."

A few minutes later I had approval for the project. In fact they said, "Go for it!"

Brimming with excitement I told Leesa what I was going to do, but beyond that I didn't say a word. The Kingdom Assignment would be a complete surprise.

Investing for the Master

Sunday finally came and I was preaching on giving God your best, whatever that might be. To illustrate the point I referred to the Parable of the Talents (Matthew 25:14–30), a story about a man who gave three of his servants varying amounts of money.

"Invest this while I'm gone," the master told them. "When I come back, I'll expect an accounting of what I gave you."

When the master returned, two faithful servants had doubled their money, causing the master great joy. The third, however, had done nothing more than bury the money. The master was very unhappy about this, took the money away from that servant, and gave it to the one who had earned the most.

"The point is this," I explained. "All we have and all we are is a gift from God. It's up to us to invest those resources in the Kingdom and watch the Master bless us in the process." I paused. My knees were quietly knocking in anticipation. "I want this to be a parable we never forget."

I was silent for a moment, watching the congregation, studying their eyes. This was it—the moment I'd waited a lifetime for. I drew a deep breath, then spoke, my voice clear and determined, yet just holding back my own excitement. "I need volunteers for a Kingdom Assignment . . ."

I'll never forget the initial response. There were nearly a thousand people in service that day and not one of them raised his or her hand. It was like looking at a herd of deer caught in the glare of a headlight. One by one I lost eye contact with nearly everyone in the first five rows as they checked their shoes or adjusted the position of their Bibles.

I cleared my throat. This was not the response I'd pictured. "I'm serious," I told them. My voice was softer than before, beseeching them to respond. "I need twenty-five volunteers." Out of four services I knew I would eventually have one hundred in all.

Slowly, uncertainly, a man halfway back rose to his feet and glanced over his shoulders. Although not another person stood, the man shuffled hesitantly forward and joined me on stage. I had tears in my eyes as he came because I believed so fully in this project and I knew—whether the man beside me did or not—that this project was going to change his life. That he'd never be the same again after that service.

The silence was so heavy it felt as though the roof had collapsed on us, and so I began to choose a few people myself and ask them to come up. At the same time, a few more got up from their seats and came forward. Finally, slowly, twenty-five people lined the stage.

I dug into my pocket and pulled out a giant fistful of money. People strained to see what I held and I waited while a hush fell over the crowd. Then I walked down the row of people and one at a time handed each of them a crisp, new $100 bill. The looks on their faces were priceless. Eyes wide, unblinking, I could almost hear some of them saying to themselves, "Okay, now he's really lost it." Several of them clearly thought it was some kind of prank or practical joke. (Later, we would find out people thought I was going to ask them to dance or reach into their own pockets and give me their money.)

Each of them held the money away from their bodies as though it might bite them. I turned to the congregation and then back to the people on stage. "Should you choose to take part in this Kingdom Assignment, it will be with these three conditions . . ."

I explained that first, they must recognize that the money did not belong to them; rather, it belonged to the Master. It was God's money.

Second, they were being trusted to invest the money in a way that would extend God's Kingdom. They could buy a homeless man dinner and a Bible or start a mission that might live on for a hundred years. Maybe they'd pay for someone's car to be fixed or purchase milk for an orphanage. I told them, "Whatever you do is between you and God."

Lastly, they must return in ninety days and share the results of their investment with the congregation.

By the end of our four services, I had given the entire $10,000 away. What had started that Sunday as fear and doubt among the people had changed to a buzz that grew with each passing hour. The hundred people had accepted my challenge, and by that evening everyone was talking about the Kingdom Assignment. Others in the congregation who hadn't come forward found those who had and added money on the spot, anxious to invest what they could in the project.

An interesting fact began to emerge as the volunteers came forward that day. These were not the standard do-gooders, the group who typically volunteered to teach Sunday school or work in the nursery. For the most part these weren't the people who gave large sums of money or were recognized as pillars of the church.

They were everyday people. People with scars and skinned hearts, deadlines and demands. Men and women who struggled at work, in their marriages, or with their children. Some participants, unbeknownst to us, were homeless! People who for the most part believed they could barely pay the bills let alone make a hundred dollars multiply for God's Kingdom.

People who struggled with fears and finances and faith.

People like me and you.

Yet on that Sunday, for some reason they were compelled to step forward and accept the assignment of a lifetime.

In Memory of Alex

Among the people who came forward that day was a man named Steve. We probably never would have known about Steve if it wasn't for the Kingdom

Assignment. But two weeks after volunteering, Steve wrote me this letter:

> *Dear Denny,*
>
> *A few weeks ago I was literally sitting in your shadow, as you stood halfway up the center aisle searching for volunteers during an early Sunday morning worship service. I sat quietly looking down, pretending to read the bulletin, while one person after another went forward. I told myself, you've found all you're looking for, I made the cut without being noticed! I looked up to my horror to see you looking straight down at me! You quietly asked if I wanted to volunteer and I was caught in your net. Before I truly knew what was happening, I had a crisp new hundred-dollar bill in my hand and, like John Belushi and Dan Ackroyd in the film The Blues Brothers, I was on a mission from God.*

The letter went on to explain the circumstances that had brought Steve to church in the first place. There was a time when he wouldn't have considered setting foot in a church, let alone accepting a Kingdom Assignment. The more Leesa and I got to know about Steve, the more sure we were that his involvement in the project was not a coincidence.

Steve came from a middle-class family in northern Wisconsin and shortly after college he took a job in business. In very little time he rocketed through multiple promotions at major companies, and by age 44 he was president of a broadcast software firm.

By then, he and his wife, Cathy, had a beautiful six-year-old daughter, Alex. Together they traveled the world, enjoying the fruits of Steve's labor. He was living the American dream until overnight his life became a nightmare.

A week after ushering in the new millennium with family and friends, Steve departed for Europe on a business trip. The first stop was London. Late the first evening, the phone rang in his hotel room. On the other end was his wife sobbing uncontrollably. Through her tears he finally realized what she was saying.

"Alex ... Alex has died."

His perfectly healthy child had died suddenly for no apparent reason while playing with a friend. In that instant Steve knew that all the power and possessions in the world were meaningless. All that mattered was the empty, aching hole that once had been filled by the charming smile and bright blue eyes of his precious little girl.

Two weeks passed and very early one Sunday morning, after crying for hours and tossing about, gripped by the talons of dark, desperate grief, Steve got up and walked through the dark house.

As he walked, he balled up his fists and pounded the walls. His tears became deep, gut-wrenching sobs. A deep sadness welled up within him, thoughts toward a God he had neither discussed nor thought about for more than two decades. "Why, God?" he shouted. "Why did You take her?"

His heart broke open like it hadn't since Alex's death, and he collapsed in a heap, weeping and begging God for understanding. Why would God's plans include the death of his little girl? "For what purpose, Lord? Why?"

The question echoed through the house again and again. Finally Steve told God that he was completely and utterly *crushed* and didn't know how he could possibly go on living. Even the simple act of breathing seemed an overwhelming and sometimes impossible chore.

"I can't go on, God. Not like this, not without her."

That's when he heard God's answer in a quiet inner voice. The whispering soothed his soul and gave him one simple direction: "Go to church."

Up until that point if you had asked Steve, he would have told you Jesus was a good man, an exceptional teacher with a powerful moral message. But the Son of God? Definitely not.

But that morning Steve was desperate, and as the sun rose he opened the telephone book and put a finger down on an ad for our church. The service times were listed, and he saw there was enough time to make the first service if he hurried. He quietly slipped into the last row of the auditorium as the service began. The message that Sunday was the first in a series titled, "Building a Case for Christ." Two months later he asked Jesus to be his personal Savior.

For the next several months, Steve attended church every week but didn't talk about his faith with anyone. He sat in the back row on the night we introduced the Kingdom Assignment. When I called him up, neither of us had any idea how this project would come to change his life.

Like all the participants, Steve took his assignment very seriously. By the time the service ended that Sunday, he was also genuinely excited about the challenge. He prayed for some time about how to use his $100 to further God's Kingdom and decided to get a few other couples in his neighborhood to join him.

Together, they planned a neighborhood Wishing Tree dedicated to the memory of his precious Alex. The goal: to fulfill the Christmas wishes of needy families in the community who otherwise would have no gifts that year.

In little time Steve collected a list of eighty wishes from three needy families, who each had several children. He wrote these wishes on paper ornaments and placed them on a large artificial Christmas tree, which they set up in a neighbor's yard.

Next, Steve and his wife distributed explanations of their project to every home in their housing development. The neighbors' response was simply overwhelming. In less than seventy-two hours, all eighty wishes were taken. God's $100 grew over the next couple of weeks to an estimated $8,000 in gifts and gift certificates for those in need, and just as important, the Kingdom Assignment touched more than one hundred neighbors who partnered in the project.

It was a Christmas Steve and his wife will never forget.

Later, reflecting on the results of his experience, Steve made some important personal discoveries. But the one that caught my attention most was captured in the closing line of another letter. "Perhaps the most profound impact from this project was that a man, after spending most of his adult life living in darkness, stepped a bit further into the light."

The amazing thing was this: Steve's story was just the beginning. Days became weeks and weeks became months, and one by one the stories flooded our office. Stories of miraculous changes and overwhelming response from strangers. Tales of hearts coming back to life and dreams coming true.

Stories that simply took our breath away.

CHAPTER 2

Changing the World with $100

As we began to hear stories of how people handled the Kingdom Assignment, a common theme appeared: Everyone who participated wanted to do their very best for Jesus. This was not only true for the hundred who accepted the challenge, but it became contagious among the congregation. What started out in our minds as being a kind of creative, outside-the-box way to teach a spiritual lesson was quickly becoming a "quest" of sorts.

And it began to take on a life of its own. A God-driven, God-powered life.

It was clear that the Kingdom Assignment was not only changing the lives of the people involved, but the very core of who we were as a community.

Terry's Story

Terry had attended our church for many years. She lived in a large home in the most affluent area of our community and drove an expensive car. She had a full-time housekeeper and was successful in everything she set her mind to accomplishing.

Most people didn't know that many years earlier Terry and her young daughter had escaped an abusive relationship. The pain of that ordeal paled, however, compared to the pain of watching her godly husband, Steve, lose his eyesight to a debilitating disease.

Steve is a successful lawyer, and, because of his blindness, Terry spends hours each day reading legal briefs aloud. In addition to that, Terry and her husband have four active children. She is a walking illustration of the Scripture, "To whom much is given, much is expected."

The day Terry received the money she tucked it away and uttered a deep and heartfelt prayer that the Lord multiply it for His glory. Later that afternoon she attended a birthday party at a local restaurant. When the guests were gathered at a long table, Terry pulled out the $100 bill and held it up.

"I got this at church today." She smiled, watching as the eyes of several people grew wide with interest.

"Isn't it supposed to work the other way around?" One of the men at the far end of the table laughed lightheartedly and waited for an explanation.

Terry smiled, sure that none of them had ever heard anything like what she was about to share. "Actually, it's a Kingdom Project. The pastor gave away $10,000 today and asked us to multiply it for God."

For a moment the room fell perfectly silent. Then one at a time the guests began to talk until the sound filled the room.

"I want to help...."

"What are you going to do...?"

"How can I get involved...?"

"Can I match it with money of my own...?"

By the time Terry left the party that night, her $100 had turned into $1800, including a free dinner donated by the restaurant. Not only did she have nearly twenty times the assignment money, she also received a tip from someone at the party as to whom she might be able to help.

One of the guests knew of a woman taking night classes at a local college and holding down two jobs. This woman had two children living with her and a third who was in a live-in recovery facility. The woman had escaped an abusive relationship, but was then assaulted and stabbed while staying at a safe house. She had been trying to make a better life for herself and her children, and the assault took what dignity she had left.

Through a series of phone calls, Terry arranged a meeting with this woman named Lisa. Though they came from different lifestyles, Terry knew they had something very special in common. They both had been abused.

The afternoon of their meeting at Terry's home, Lisa knocked tentatively on the door of what probably looked to her like a mansion. A warm, outgoing woman answered the door, and the awkwardness between them lasted only a moment before Terry rushed into Lisa's arms. "Hi, Lisa," Terry said, her voice thick with emotion. "God has brought us together because He wants us to be friends."

The money raised at that Sunday afternoon birthday party allowed Terry to help Lisa with her rent. In addition, Terry purchased gift certificates for Lisa and her children to help them get through Christmas. Not long after Terry made her delivery she received a call from Lisa.

"There was some money left over," she said, joy ringing in her voice. "Me and the kids bought some presents for some other children we know. Children with far less than us."

Terry listened as tears filled her eyes. Only God, she reasoned, could design a project that allowed a single $100 bill to keep giving and giving.

The more time Terry spent with Lisa the more she saw that though they had nothing in common on the surface, there were things they could learn from each other—lessons about everything from their children's schooling to the difficulties of trusting again after living in an abusive relationship.

Terry and Steve were able to help Lisa with her legal problems concerning her middle child, and in a matter of weeks the two families began attending church together. Someone from the congregation offered to care for Lisa's eight-year-old daughter after school while Lisa worked. A fund was created to purchase a computer for her oldest son so he could compete with other students vying for college scholarships.

And God wasn't finished yet.

When long lost relatives of Lisa saw a story about her and the Kingdom Project in a local newspaper, they contacted her and a reunion was staged. "What can we do to help?" they wanted to know. They started making plans that day to take Lisa under their care.

"I don't understand about the project," one of Lisa's relatives said. "But I know this. Lisa will never be without family again because of it."

Kim's Story

Kim was a single woman who had a heart that beat strongly for children. When she received her $100, she knew one thing only. She didn't want to simply hand it over to a person or organization. Instead, she wanted to experience firsthand what that money could do for God's Kingdom.

And deep in her soul she knew the investment would have something to do with children.

It was not a coincidence when later that week Kim was having dinner with a friend and the topic of the local children's hospital came up.

"I'm taking a children's literature class," the friend explained. She moved her straw about in her drink. When she looked up, Kim saw tears well up in her friend's eyes. "We're supposed to read to sick kids in the hospital." There was silence for a moment. "I keep thinking how sad it is that they have nothing else to look forward to. Nothing but the treasure of hearing a simple story between hospital procedures."

The next morning Kim woke up and realized, "That's it!" She formulated a plan and dedicated it to God, and that day she visited a few bookstores to ask if they would match her $100. The responses came quicker than expected. Everyone wanted to help, and God was answering prayers in a way she had never seen before. In the past it seemed she had to wait to hear God's answers. Now it appeared God was answering prayers moment by moment. Before she could begin to visit some children at the hospital, Kim was beginning to see her donated library grow.

Kim contacted more bookstores in the area and arranged for them to donate books not just for sick kids at the hospital but also for a teen shelter in Laguna Beach. At the end of the month she had received more than two hundred donated books.

Then something unexpected happened. Kim worked as a customer service representative for a freight and shipping company. She was working one afternoon when she received a call from a man who was obviously upset. He was not satisfied with the equipment her company had provided for him.

"I need someone to come pick this junk up and get me my money back!" he demanded. "Then you can cancel my contract."

Kim said a silent prayer and drew a deep breath. "I'm very sorry, sir. Let's see if we can't try and work through this." She asked what kind of product he shipped.

"Books," he snapped. "Children's books."

Kim's heart skipped a beat. "Sir, I know you're upset right now and . . . well . . . this is going to sound very strange, but I have a story to tell you. . . ."

Then she told the stranger on the phone a summary of the Kingdom Assignment and what had happened since she had invested her $100 in children's books for sick and needy children.

There was silence on the other end. "Are you still there?" she asked.

"Okay," he said sheepishly. "I'll give your company another chance." He hesitated and his voice grew thick. "And you can send someone to pick up as many books as you want from my warehouse. It's filled with children's books."

And so Kim collected hundreds more books for children.

Kim was now ready for the second part of her assignment. She called and got permission from the director of the children's hospital, drove there one afternoon, said a prayer in her car, and then headed in. Her first stop was the recreation room where she'd been told that terminally sick children spent most of their time. She saw the monitors on which the kids watched cartoons or played video games. She imagined that as they played, they'd talk about wanting to quickly return to their own homes and neighborhoods to be with their school friends, where life was normal. Where there were no needles and medicines, no long names of diseases, and no crying by Mommy and Daddy.

Kim knew it was important to stay enthusiastic and positive, but in her heart she had to fight back tears as she walked over to two pajama-clothed ten-year-old girls. "Hi, girls," she said, feeling the words catch in her throat and echo in the hollow, sterile room.

The girls swung around and simply said, "Hi." The mother of one leaned ever so slightly toward them, wondering what Kim would do next. As she made her way over to a chair too small for her, Kim looked at the girls and paused, taking a deep breath. "I've been a part of a wonderful event at my church," Kim said, her eyes glistening.

The mother began to relax as she listened to Kim's story. "I read about that in the newspaper," the mom remarked. Kim said, "My assignment is to read you some stories. Could I do that?" The girls brightened up a bit, nodded, and moved a little closer together, getting comfortable as they prepared to listen. Kim pulled a book from her bag, which was a story of the ins and outs of life as a ten-year-old girl. The girls sat wide-eyed, hanging on her every word.

When Kim finished the story, she gave each girl her own book to keep. "God bless you," she said as she gave them a hug. The room seemed brighter as she waved good–bye and stepped out of the recreation area. The girls were still holding onto their books. And Mommy wasn't crying.

As Kim shared this story with me, her entire face glowed with the certainty of knowing she'd accomplished what was asked of her in the Kingdom Assignment. Then she told me this: "I've always wondered what God wanted me to do with my life and I was never quite sure." She blinked back tears. "Today I know for sure. I'm starting an organization that will see to it that there are always ample books for children like my ten-year-old friends. And one day, when I have my own children, I'll pass this Kingdom Assignment on to them."

Brooks's Story

Brooks wanted to be involved in his son's life. The chance came along when his young son showed some interest in becoming a Cub Scout. Brooks knew the Scouting program was a great way to grow up. He volunteered and became a leader of his son's pack. He and his son earned badges together, and he watched as his son matured and moved from Cub to Boy Scout. The troop he led was thriving and successful, one of the strongest within their community. He had his hands so full with his own troop that understandably he had little time or interest in helping other troops in the area. That is, until he volunteered for something else called the Kingdom Assignment.

When he took hold of the $100 bill that Sunday, he felt deep in his being that God wanted him to use it to help children grow up with the Boy Scouts' discipline and love for God, family, and country.

A few weeks into the assignment, Brooks received a phone call from a friend who'd heard about the project.

"This may be your answer," the friend said. "There are kids not thirty minutes from here who get together once in a while but can't afford to form a Cub Scout Troop."

"They can't afford a place to meet?" Brooks grabbed a pencil and began taking notes.

"No, Brooks. They can't afford the $5 handbook."

At the next Boy Scout meeting Brooks set a bowl in the middle of the room and explained about the less fortunate children across town who couldn't afford to be Cub Scouts. He pointed to the bowl. "That's a special bowl because..." he tossed in his hundred-dollar bill, "when God's Kingdom is at stake, it has a way of multiplying the money inside."

One by one parents of the Scouts began tossing in money. A fellow Scout parent matched it with his own $100 bill. Two weeks later they had raised enough money not only to give all the boys handbooks, but uniforms as well. That's when Brooks's heard about Anthony. The child had dreamed of being a Cub Scout all his life. The day Brooks and his troop took the supplies to the grateful boys across town was one Brooks will never forget.

Anthony thanked the boys from Brooks's troop and then hurriedly took his uniform into a nearby bathroom. When he came out, he was beaming with a smile broader than any Brooks had seen. "I just want you to know," Anthony said as he raised a fist in the air. "This is the best day of my whole life."

Craig's Story

Craig is a chiropractor by trade, but he's better known for his servant heart than his back adjustments. You could ask anything of Craig and he'd find a way to get it for you. What most people didn't know was that Craig was in a slump. Things at home had become a chore and his spiritual life was dry and disjointed. He knew he needed to be involved somewhere, bearing fruit. Everything in his life had become routine. He wasn't sleeping well, and even fun evenings with the family had gone by the wayside. The worst part was he didn't seem to care. He knew he was settling for second best in his life. But to take a risk, well, "that was just too much work." I could tell he felt a little irritated when I nudged him to get on the stage during the service. He was comfortable going to the same service and sitting in the same seat every week.

That was about to change.

"Why me, God?" he asked the Lord in the days after accepting the assignment. "I can't even get things right at home. How can I do anything for Your Kingdom with $100?"

The response echoed deep in his spirit. *Pray*, God clearly told him. *Pray and the idea will come.*

And so Craig prayed. When he wasn't praying, he asked around and thought up ways to make his $100 go as far as possible for the Lord. Then one day he was contacted by a friend who worked at an inner-city mission.

"Why don't you use the money to start a program down here," the friend suggested. "You have no idea how much they need."

Craig hesitated and started to tell the friend he wasn't up for the task, and that he couldn't possibly help people in the inner-city if he couldn't first help the people at his kitchen table. But when he opened his mouth he found himself agreeing.

In no time Craig and his friend set the plan in action. That weekend the two men purchased $100 of hot hamburgers, took them to a skid-row section of Los Angeles, and set up a chiropractic table on the urine-soaked sidewalk.

It took a while for the idea to spread, but one by one homeless people began lining up at the table, accepting a complete back adjustment and a warm meal in the name of Christ. Near the end of the afternoon, Craig adjusted the back of one particularly old man, an alcoholic dressed in rags, who he was sure had spent his share of nights underneath the freeway overpass.

There were tears streaming down the man's face as he held out his hand to Craig. "Sir, I don't know who you are or where you come from. But I haven't felt this good in ten years."

Immediately Craig pictured the lepers who must have felt that way when Jesus walked the earth. He struggled to find his voice. "Don't thank me," Craig smiled and pointed toward heaven. "Thank God. I'm on assignment for Him."

When Craig got home that day, he shared the day's adventure with his wife and sons. For the first time in what seemed like years, they spent an evening laughing and loving like the family they'd once been.

A month later Craig went back to the same spot and did the same thing again, this time taking his two young sons with him. As the weeks went by, the enthusiasm for life Craig had once known came back to him.

Today they are a different family because of what the Kingdom Assignment has done to their hearts. And the chiropractic hamburger ministry? It continues on. Craig has committed to carrying out the assignment for at least a year, and after that? There truly are no limits to what God might do.

Julie's Story

When I presented the Kingdom Assignment that Sunday, Julie had no intention of participating. If it weren't for the fact that I didn't have enough volunteers, she never would have been involved. But there I was wandering the center aisle looking for people to take on the project when my eyes fell on her.

Her heart raced within her and sweat broke out on her brow. She had no intention of being involved, but when I called her name, she reluctantly came forward.

"Okay, God," she whispered as she returned to her seat. "Show me what this is all about."

She spent almost two months praying about what God wanted her to do with the money. There were many nights when she lay awake unable to sleep, imagining why God had wanted her among the participants and wondering what she should do with His money.

"You know me," she told her husband one morning. "If I'm going to invest it in God's Kingdom, I want to really make a difference."

Her husband thought for a moment and then blurted out the name of a friend Julie had gone to high school with. "Didn't she start that organization ... you know, Project Cuddle? Maybe you could invest the money there."

Julie's mind began to race. The idea was interesting. Project Cuddle was a national organization aimed at pregnant women who might otherwise abandon their babies to doorsteps or dumpsters.

Julie gave her friend a call.

"Why don't you use the money to print brochures for Project Cuddle," the friend suggested. "That would help."

"Hmm," Julie closed her eyes, trying to hear God's leading in what she believed to be a crucial decision. "I was thinking of something more personal."

"Wait! I've got it!" Her friend's voice was shrill with enthusiasm.

"There's a girl who's been on my heart for a very long time. Her name is Reyna . . ."

Thirty minutes later Julie felt as though she knew Reyna personally. The woman had been rejected by her family for being pregnant. She was unmarried and without a friend in the world.

Hope and assurance flooded Julie's heart. "That's it! She's the one I'm supposed to help."

Phone calls were made. Within a week Julie met Reyna and they became the most unlikely friends: a young woman from South Central Los Angeles and a woman from affluent Orange County with one thing in common—the Kingdom Assignment.

"I'd like to throw you a baby shower," Julie told Reyna as their friendship grew. "Give me a list of everything you need."

Reyna was taken back. "How could you do this for me—someone you don't even know?" Reyna's eyes quickly filled with tears as Julie expressed concern for

her by reaching out and showing her God's uncondi-
tional love.

"I have been so alone," Reyna said. "I now have
hope I didn't have yesterday. I don't know how I could
ever thank you."

There was no need in Julie's mind, of course. She
had followed God's leading and her heart was filled
with thankfulness also, having already received more
than she had given or would give in the future.

Later that month after much organization, Julie
threw Reyna a baby shower she'll never forget. Some
fifty women—more than were invited—attended the
shower and brought Reyna a complete baby wardrobe
and all the necessities a first-time mother might need.
Reyna looked radiant. Throughout the shower she held
her hand protectively against her protruding belly. "My
baby is loved," she kept saying. "My baby is loved."

Michael's Story

Before taking on the Kingdom Assignment, Michael
rarely took the time to consider those less fortunate
than him. He grew up in a neighborhood that offered
little opportunity to learn skills or become successful
in society, but he became an honor student, a star ath-
lete, and eventually a successful businessman. He was
on a fast track and had designed a world around himself that was contained and in control. If he'd seen

someone like sixteen-year-old Mateo walking on the street, he would barely have noticed that when this typical teenager smiled, he had no teeth.

But God had a plan to change all that.

The day the project was announced, Michael volunteered because he thought the assignment was some sort of game. Although he'd been a believer for a few years, he'd kept his faith to himself as sort of a handy addition when he needed help in a jam. As he walked up to the stage to accept the assignment, his faith was the furthest thing from his mind. Rather, he sort of enjoyed the attention and figured it might be his chance to ham up the project a bit and win a few laughs.

When he realized what the Kingdom Assignment was about, his attitude changed completely. "Why did I volunteer for this set?" he grumbled to his friend later. "I should've just stayed in my seat."

As he left church that Sunday, he figured he'd give the $100 bill to the first homeless person he saw and that would be the end of it. But to no avail. The $100 bill remained in his wallet, like a haunt every time he went to pay for McDonald's or a bunch of bananas at the grocery store.

"You're letting that $100 eat you alive, Michael," his wife told him one day a month later. "You need to invest it in something." She paused. "By the way, I have an idea . . ."

Michael's wife, Helen, worked for the Red Cross, and she knew of a family who had lost a child earlier that year to a rare disease called a-plastic anemia. "I don't know, honey," she said as they ate dinner that night. "Maybe there's something you can do to help."

Having nothing else to go on, Michael looked into it and found out that this family had not only lost their nine-year-old daughter but six days prior to his call had lost their sixteen-year-old daughter to the same disease. That is, they lost both children within months of each other, and they had no funds to pay for a funeral for either child.

Then Michael learned about Mateo, their only surviving child. He was a sophomore in high school and was experiencing terrible effects from another debilitating disease. The illness had caused him to lose all his teeth.

"What's being done to help them?" Michael asked the caseworker. He began to feel overwhelming emotions toward people he didn't even know and waited breathlessly for the response.

The caseworker sighed. "I'm afraid there's nothing we can do. We're completely out of funds." The woman's voice broke. "In fact, I was praying for a miracle for this family just this morning."

Michael was inspired but he knew he had a great deal of work ahead of him. In the hours that followed his decision to help Mateo and his family, he felt as though he'd gone straight to God and said, "Put me in, Coach, I'm ready to play!"

In the days ahead, Michael spoke to his coworkers, who began to match his $100. Challenges went out to old roommates from college and fraternity buddies. He enthusiastically told the story of how he received this assignment. He also told of this family, their deep grief, and their surviving son, Mateo. Michael became impassioned about this cause.

If people didn't know he was a Christian before, they did now.

The response was more than Michael could have dared dream. People not only sent money, they sent it cheerfully and tearfully, until finally Michael had more than one hundred times the original $100. In the process, Michael became a fully committed believer. And for the first time, he led a coworker to a new relationship with God through Jesus Christ.

"I'm a child of the King," Michael says when people ask. "Everything I do, everything I am is part of being in the Kingdom of God, on assignment for Him."

One more thing.

On the night of our church's celebration for what God was doing, a plea went out concerning Mateo's increasing dental costs. A dentist in the audience quickly realized he had found *his* assignment. Mateo would soon have a full set of teeth!

Through all the rewards that have come from being a participant in the Kingdom Assignment, the greatest for Michael was the day he visited Mateo after his oral surgery. The smile Mateo gave him that afternoon is one Michael will remember for the rest of his life.

Mike's Story

The darkest moment in Mike's life happened years before he accepted the Kingdom Assignment. Discouragement and despair from a lifetime of abuse ran through Mike's veins like a deadly drug back then. One night he bought a gun, loaded all six chambers with bullets, and buried his head under a pillow to muffle the sound.

Then he pulled the trigger.

He felt the hammer on the gun land, but the gun did not go off. He knew every chamber was loaded, so there was no reason for the gun not to work. Frustrated he opened the barrel to see what was wrong, and a single bullet fell out on his lap.

For nearly a minute he stared at the bullet as gradually he began to realize a miracle had taken place.

This is not your time, Mike, he heard God tell him. *Not today, not like this.*

That was the beginning of his recovery. Eventually his path to healing led him to our church, where he got involved in a mentoring relationship with one of the other men in the congregation. The man shared hope from Scripture and helped him find joy in living again.

"You helped save my life," he told the mentor friend one day shortly before the Kingdom Assignment was handed out. "If I ever have the chance, I'm going to help others the way you've helped me."

Those words came back to him as he stood up on the stage and accepted his $100 assignment. Before he got back to his seat he knew what God was calling him to do. The next morning he did some research and learned of an organization called Mentor Me, responsible for pairing up members of the community with troubled boys and girls. The program had experienced great success and Mike knew without a doubt this was where God would have him invest.

Especially after God had saved his life through the mentoring of someone else.

He phoned the organization and offered two things: the $100 bill and his time as a volunteer mentor to young people with similar traumatic childhood experiences.

"God gave me my life back," Mike told me later. "If I can use the Kingdom Assignment to help someone like I used to be find life again, then without a doubt I'm the one who's blessed. Again and again."

For far too many, the church is seen as a "closed community," a "holy huddle" of believers, who are seen by outsiders as indifferent to their various plights or hypocritical in their actions. Jesus told His disciples, "You are the light of the world," a "city on a hill" that was never meant to be hidden from sight, but put on a stand for "everyone to see."

And how?

Not just by *speaking* the gospel, but also by living it out. Jesus also said, "In the same way, let your light shine before men, that they may see your good deeds and praise your Father in heaven" (Matthew 5:16).

If the truth were told, we are missing countless simple opportunities everyday to display the gospel. Opportunities that demonstrate the light of Christ, the truth of Christ, the character of Christ, and the Kingdom of Christ. Opportunities that don't demand $100, but do demand a Kingdom investment-minded strategy that needs to be understood and put into practice.

These Kingdom Assignment participants took the project seriously and made a decision to multiply their investment. They chose to bring practical and spiritual help to a world that needs to see the church, not just hear from the church.

And that's exactly what they did. The dividends that came as a result are still growing and include the following:

- books for the lonely
- blankets for the homeless
- countless prayers and acts of kindness for people outside the church
- Bibles for the spiritually hungry
- food for the physically hungry
- gifts and gift certificates for people with no means
- dreams and hopes realized
- computers for those who can support themselves as a result
- care packages
- overseas help
- assistance for the *Jesus* Film Project
- hours of ministry service
- clothing and greeting cards to the sick
- works of art, sculptures sold for donation to the local children's hospital
- breakfast for men learning how to be better husbands
- homes for homeless families in Mexico
- grief packets for those who miscarried or lost infants

- assistance to unwed mothers
- medical equipment for those without
- camp scholarships for needy children
- a home for Chinese seminary students in China
- assistance to a prison ministry
- a table for a family who had nowhere to sit at mealtime
- a bone marrow drive
- and many, many more

CHAPTER 3

"The Most Important $100 I've Ever Held"

I can still remember the first time in my life that I actually held a $100 bill. It was Christmas Day, 1977. Leesa and I were home on vacation for the holidays from grad school, and as is often the case with seminarians, money was tight.

On this particular Christmas morning, we had just opened our gifts and the nephews were playing loudly with their latest toy, when Leesa's father, Chick Saffell, pulled two gifts from the closet for me and my brother-in-law. We opened them and found thin windbreakers inside.

As we tried them on he commented that they did have a slight flaw in the pockets. I smiled politely but have to admit, on the inside, I was thinking "that's nice." When I reached into the pockets on either side of the jacket, sure enough, there appeared to be a problem. Something was bunched up inside them. It felt like crumpled paper, and when I pulled it out of my pockets to see what in fact was there, I was stunned.

The crumpled paper was five $100 bills. When I realized what he'd done I almost lost my breath. Leesa, on the other hand, let out a loud scream! We had never seen that much money in our young lives, let alone held it. It was, and remains to this day, a very special memory.

A $100 Bill Isn't Much

Since that day I have, like most of you, held in my hands several $100 bills and thought nothing of it. Call it inflation. Call it affluence. Call it a normal occurrence in our present society. I would imagine holding a $100 bill for the most part isn't that big of a deal.

Think about the ways you spend $100 without blinking an eye.

- two tanks of gas for your sports utility vehicle
- three bags of groceries
- dinner, a movie, and five hours of babysitting
- one week's worth of electricity
- a quick stop at Wal-Mart

At first glance $100 really isn't that much. Unless, of course, you thought and believed it belonged to God.

We found out the week after I gave the Kingdom Assignment that handing out $100 bills created some very interesting reactions among those who received them. While there was definitely a buzz among the congregation about their excitement toward this Kingdom Assignment, there was also a growing sense of responsibility among the participants.

I started to get calls from some who told me they weren't sleeping at night thinking about the responsibility of what they were going to do with "God's money."

Bill, a $100 recipient and successful businessman in our community, approached me in church the following Sunday to thank me for the opportunity and to tell me in no uncertain terms, *"This is the most significant $100 I have ever held in my life."*

Over and over again people were telling me this and others variations on the same theme. I knew this would be exciting for the church, and I knew it would be perceived as a learning experience for those who participated, but what I didn't realize was how serious people would be in taking it to heart.

This was not just any $100. This money belonged to the Lord, and He had entrusted them to invest it as they saw best to expand God's Kingdom, to glorify God in some way, and to benefit others. Wow! Something big was happening.

People were beginning to think like the "stewards" God says they are instead of "owners" this world says they should strive to be. Imagine what would happen if Christians everywhere began to think and act like that. It would change their lives . . . and likely the lives of countless people around them. This is exactly what God wants to do . . . change the world one person at a time.

And He wants to use you to help do it.

You say, "But what can a measly $100 do to change the world?" More than you can ever imagine in the eyes and hands of people determined to make a worthwhile investment for God.

Taking the Challenge to Heart

If you were to meet Doug and know him as I have come to do in the last year, there are a couple of things that would jump out at you. One is his good business sense. In the business world of South Orange County, California, Doug is known as a leader, a winner, a man of great integrity and success, and a man with impeccable ethical credentials. In business, when Doug talks, people listen. He's a "player." The other thing you might notice, however, is his rather quiet and shy way about his newfound faith. When Doug received his $100 bill, it became more than a mere note of currency. It became an opportunity to be spiritually bold in a way he hadn't been before.

Together, he and his wife, Kathryn, began to pray and ask God what He wanted them to do with the $100 of God's money. The answer they got was "make it grow." Doug decided to be bold. He wrote a letter to ten guys who had all been fraternity brothers of his in college twenty-five years earlier. In that letter, he got real and told them that he had become a Christian, was attending a church, and was involved in a men's Bible study. He also told them of his "assignment" and asked them to join him.

Wanting to get the biggest bang for his buck, he prayerfully decided he would invest his $100 with the *Jesus* Film Project, a division of Campus Crusade for Christ. This film has captured the Gospel of Luke, and Campus Crusade has translated it into over 700 different languages and dialects around the world in an attempt to share the gospel with every person of every people group on the planet before the return of the Lord. It has also been effective in beginning new churches in Third World countries around the world.

When Doug declared his intentions to his friends, he asked if they would match the $100 and that he would match the cumulative total of the group and make a donation to the *Jesus* Film Project. The response was remarkable. Virtually everyone in the group responded favorably. In fact one man sent him $5,000. Another told him that he was the last person he ever expected to receive such a letter and request from, but he gladly made a contribution.

The most dramatic response, however, came from a friend who was and remains an atheist. He wrote back and declined Doug's request. "My wife is a Christian," he told Doug in his rejection letter. "I value a person having a choice in these matters. But I've made my choice based on my convictions and regret to tell you I cannot participate."

Undaunted, Doug wrote back and told his friend that having a choice was exactly why he chose to invest in the *Jesus* Film Project. His goal was to help people who had never had a chance to hear about Jesus so that they could make an informed choice of their own. Remarkably, Doug's friend wrote back a note saying he thought he had a "good point," and he appreciated the effort. A seed was planted that will grow in ways Doug may never know.

From his ten letters, Doug collected over $6,000, which he and Kathryn matched and gave to the *Jesus* Film Project.

But that only tells half the story.

You have to know what that $13,000 meant to the *Jesus* Film Project. A few years ago I traveled to Africa with the director of the *Jesus* Film Project, Paul Eshleman. While there I got to see firsthand the efforts and effects of showing this film.

"What can $13,000 do for your organization?" I asked Paul.

He told me that $13,000 would support two African nationals for a year, supplying them with a copy of the *Jesus* film, a projector, a screen, a portable generator, and gas to show that movie some three days a week for one full year.

A donation that size would mean more than 200,000 people would see the *Jesus* film. Statistics showed that during that time several *dozen* churches would most likely be formed as well.

What can $100 really accomplish?

In this case more than 130 times the financial investment, and immeasurably more in lives changed both for today and for eternity.

You see, this assignment isn't about money. It never was, and never will be. It's about faithfully using anything and everything God has given us in a way that will expand His Kingdom and bring Him glory.

CHAPTER 4

Whose Stuff Is It Anyway?

Over the years my wife and I have made lots of mistakes with money, and my guess is you have too. The important thing is we're still learning. Sometimes we learn the hard way, but we're learning just the same.

A few months back we were late on a bill. We had the money, mind you, and every intention of paying on time, but in our forgetfulness, or laziness (or whatever you want to call it), we overlooked it. As a result, we were issued a $200 late fee. Two hundred dollars! If we hadn't experienced this Kingdom Assignment, I doubt if it would have affected us as harshly as it did.

But now we *know* what $100 can mean and do, let alone $200.

Why All That Talk About Money?

Have you ever wondered why Jesus talked so much about money? Lots of people like to think that money is talked about too much in the church. The truth is, it's probably not talked about nearly enough, at least not in the way that Jesus did. In his ministry, Jesus talked about money more than just about any other subject, and I think I know why. There are two main reasons.

The first is because nothing gets our attention in this life quite like money does. Have you noticed that? I heard a story awhile back about a man who called a church and asked to speak to the "head hog in the trough." The receptionist was indignant. "If you're speaking of our senior pastor," she shot back, "I'll have you know we have a bit more respect for him than that. But just the same, he's not in his office right now. Would you like me to have him call you when he returns?"

The man apologized, "I'm sorry, I just wanted to stop by and give him a check for $25,000 my wife and I wanted to donate to the church." To which the receptionist replied, "Just a minute, I think I see the *Big Pig* coming through the door right now!"

Nothing gets our attention quite like money does, even in the first century, and I think Jesus knew that.

The other reason I believe Jesus spoke so much about money is because this subject is a very spiritual issue. Jesus said, "Where your treasure [money] is, there your heart will be also" (Matthew 6:21). Know why? Money not only calls for our attention, it also calls for our hearts, our allegiance, our devotion, just as God does. In fact, the Bible says there is something about money that *rivals* God. Think about it. Money has many of the same qualities we attribute to God. It creates, it provides, it protects, it controls.

Money, we say, is the bottom line. And to some degree it is. This is exactly why Jesus said, "You cannot serve both God and Money" (Matthew 6:24). It's true, isn't it? We can either use our money to serve God or our god *will be* our money. They will always vie for preeminence in our lives. The question is, who is going to win the battle for our hearts?

A Radical Change in Thinking

I believe that Jesus talked frequently about money because He knew nothing could take us away from Him more quickly than our bank accounts. The apostle Paul echoed the same message for the young Christian church when he wrote:

> For the love of money is a root of all kinds of evil. Some
> people, eager for money, have wandered from the faith
> and pierced themselves with many griefs.
>
> 1 TIMOTHY 6:10

His solution to this dilemma, however, is also spelled out:

> Command those who are rich in this present world not to be arrogant nor to put their hope in wealth, which is so uncertain, but to put their hope in God, who richly provides us with everything for our enjoyment. Command them to do good, to be rich in good deeds, and to be generous and willing to share. In this way they will lay up treasure for themselves as a firm foundation for the coming age, so that they may take hold of the life that is truly life.
>
> 1 TIMOTHY 6:17–19

The answer, Paul says, lies in a personal paradigm shift in money matters, a radical change in thinking and acting toward one's understanding and relationship with money. A shift away from *loving* money to *using* money in ways that demonstrate one's love and devotion and service to God and to His purpose.

I think that's what Jesus was attempting to teach His disciples in the Parable of the Talents (Matthew 25:14–30), which became the launching pad for this Kingdom Assignment.

> 14Again, it will be like a man going on a journey, who called his servants and entrusted his property to them. 15To one he gave five talents of money, to another

two talents, and to another one talent, each according to his ability. Then he went on his journey. ¹⁶The man who had received the five talents went at once and put his money to work and gained five more. ¹⁷So also, the one with the two talents gained two more. ¹⁸But the man who had received the one talent went off, dug a hole in the ground and hid his master's money.

¹⁹After a long time the master of those servants returned and settled accounts with them. ²⁰The man who had received the five talents brought the other five. "Master," he said, "you entrusted me with five talents. See, I have gained five more."

²¹His master replied, "Well done, good and faithful servant! You have been faithful with a few things; I will put you in charge of many things. Come and share your master's happiness!"

²²The man with the two talents also came. "Master," he said, "you entrusted me with two talents; see, I have gained two more."

²³His master replied, "Well done, good and faithful servant! You have been faithful with a few things; I will put you in charge of many things. Come and share your master's happiness!"

²⁴Then the man who had received the one talent came. "Master," he said, "I knew that you are a hard man, harvesting where you have not sown and gathering where you have not scattered seed. ²⁵ So I was afraid

and went out and hid your talent in the ground. See, here is what belongs to you."

²⁶His master replied, "You wicked, lazy servant! So you knew that I harvest where I have not sown and gather where I have not scattered seed? ²⁷Well then, you should have put my money on deposit with the bankers, so that when I returned I would have received it back with interest.

²⁸ "Take the talent from him and give it to the one who has the ten talents. ²⁹For everyone who has will be given more, and he will have an abundance. Whoever does not have, even what he has will be taken from him. ³⁰And throw that worthless servant outside, into the darkness, where there will be weeping and gnashing of teeth."

The teaching of the Parable of the Talents actually takes place in the context of Jesus' teaching about the end times and His eventual return. One of the prevailing questions for consideration is, *Will the Lord find faithful servants at the time of his coming?*

This is the focus of Jesus' three parables in Matthew 25: the Parable of the Ten Virgins, the Parable of the Talents, and the Parable of the Sheep and Goats. The Parable of the Talents teaches three significant principles if we intend to be successful in our Kingdom Assignment.

The Principle of Personal Management

For years I used to think that stewardship was solely about giving, in particular, giving money to the church. Unfortunately, annual stewardship campaigns in the church only tend to reinforce that misconception. Now, don't get me wrong; I am not against giving to the church at all. In fact, as a senior pastor I make it a point to teach the regular practice of giving as a personal discipline of authentic, devoted followers of Jesus and as a characteristic of a *faithful steward*.

But stewardship is not essentially about giving. Giving is something a faithful steward *does*. Stewardship is rather about living all of life believing everything you are and everything you have belongs first and foremost to God.

There is also another life focus that competes with that of stewardship. The countermind-set of stewardship is ownership. Both of these focus on how we view ourselves and, as a result, how we live accordingly.

If we view ourselves as *owners*, we will live with a certain set of values. If we view ourselves as *stewards*, we will likely live with another set of values. For instance, many people celebrate the day they pay off their cars and are finally able to get the prized pink slip. From that day on you own the car; it's yours and not something you share with a bank.

Owners value taking possession of, holding title to, and having control over. And the more possessions one amasses, the more property one takes title to, and the more things one maintains control over, the more powerful an owner one becomes.

Stewards, on the other hand, value a different set of things. For instance, stewards take joy not in what they possess, but in what they have been entrusted with; not in how much they lay title to, but in what they have access to use; and not in what they control, but in what they have available at any one time to manage most effectively on the owner's behalf and in the owner's best interests.

A steward would pay off his vehicle and say, "I wonder what God would have me do with the extra money each month now that the car is paid off."

Ownership is a tremendous value in the society we live in as Americans. In fact, it is part of our American dream. Interestingly, however, it's *not* particularly a value for people in the Kingdom of God. Know why? Because in the Kingdom, ownership is the sole privilege of the King. It all *belongs* to Him. The good news is, as Christians, we serve a benevolent King, who has graciously *entrusted us* with every good gift and made them available to us to enjoy, to use, and to manage in any number of creative ways we choose on His behalf and with His good purpose in mind. This is one of the keys to understanding this parable. It comes down to how we perceive ourselves—as stewards or owners.

The Principle of Excellence

Not only did the master entrust his property to the servants, Jesus said, but he distributed differing measures of "talents" to them. Now, a talent in this context is a *measure* or a *weight* of something. In this particular case, it was a measure of money. To one, as the story goes, the master gave five talents, to another two talents, and to still another he gave one talent.

Each one was entrusted with a very gracious gift that belonged to the master and was told to put it to work for him and his estate until he returned. Immediately, we're told, the servants with five and two talents gave themselves to the effort of enthusiastically putting their talents to work, investing it in the best interest of their master. One, however, buried his talent. The principle of excellence has to do with giving God your best. Your best effort ... in the best interests of the Master. It has to do with honor.

Awhile back in my own life, I sensed God wanting me to raise the bar on my personal understanding of what it meant to honor Him. Essentially, it was about exploring ways for me to continue to make God a more constant part of my life, both in my thoughts and actions. And frankly, I found myself somewhat hesitant. The reason, I determined, was because I was comfortable with things the way they were. Too comfortable, it seemed. You see, I have a tendency to get lazy when I'm too comfortable, to settle for the status quo, even mediocrity. And mediocrity is not honoring to God.

Now, some of us have the idea that excellence is some perfectionist ordeal. No, perfectionism is a sickness that constrains our efforts and our joy. The pursuit of excellence is having an ideal and giving your best in the pursuit of it. In this case, it means taking what God has given us and investing it with our best efforts, not burying it in the ground.

I think most of us realize that mediocrity isn't worth much in our personal or professional lives. I don't know anybody who says, "You know, in my personal life, my ultimate goal is to be as mediocre as I can be." I don't know anybody in business who says, "You know, here's the goal of our company, to be mediocre." They don't do that, and yet somehow it seems that we're easily ready to accept mediocrity in our spiritual life as almost a goal. Because, after all, we don't want to make too much of this God-thing. What would people think? What would people say?

The truth is they just might say, "Look at him! Look at her! I think they're actually serious about all this Christianity stuff."

That's what often happened to the Israelites. They forgot about excellence, and they did so several times over the course of their history. On the other side of the Red Sea they forgot who they were as the people of God. They forgot *whose* they were. They forgot history—their history—and what God had done for them. In addition, they forgot what God had called them to be.

Do you remember what God called His people to do in the Old Testament? He said He had chosen them to serve as a channel of God's blessing to the rest of the world . . . to be a light to the Gentiles. They forgot that, and what they didn't realize was that while they were doing so, they were cheating God out of what He really deserved. Honor . . . and their *best efforts* to honor Him.

The Principle of Accountability

The sobering part of the Parable of the Talents is that Jesus says, after a long time, the master of those servants returned and "settled accounts with them" (Matthew 25:19). To those who had invested wisely, he rewarded. To the one who buried his talent, he judged. Severely. In fact, the master took the talent that had been hidden in the ground away from the "wicked servant" and gave it to the one who had seen the greatest return on his investment. The point here is, when it comes to the gifts God distributes, either we *use* them or *lose* them.

The choice is ours.

I remember the following weekend after we passed out the $100 bills there was an aura of anticipation around our church. People were already starting to talk about it and to look with enthusiastic anticipation on what was going to be the outcome. A number of folks called to tell me they wished they could have been part of the assignment. Others said if they had only known what I was going to ask them to do, they would have loved to be a part of it. My response to them was, "You *can* be part of it."

In fact, it's the same answer I give you, here and now. The truth is, God has entrusted every one of us with a lot more than $100. The question is, do we see it as such? Will we honor God with it? And how will we do so?

Think with me a minute about this parable. Do you realize what could happen if every follower of Christ began to think and act in line with these principles that Jesus taught? Imagine what could happen if every Christ follower began to see himself or herself as a steward instead of an owner. If every Christ follower began to be mindful and purposeful about investing in God's Kingdom and agenda instead of simply his or her own. If every Christ follower thought and acted consciously knowing that one day God is going to settle accounts with us regarding all He has entrusted to us. It would more than likely change our lives . . . and just as likely, the lives of others around us.

Which is exactly what God desires to do.

CHAPTER 5

What's in This for You?

When it was all over and the last report had been shared before the crowd of two thousand people and members of the media, Leesa asked all hundred participants to make their way to the center aisle. She asked the rest of the congregation of observers to come to the center and place their hands on the shoulders of those volunteers. As I surveyed the sanctuary I was overcome with emotion. Then, through my tears, I spoke the words I hope to hear Jesus say one day about me.

"Well done, good and faithful servants."

I saw the faces of so many who stood before me who had accomplished so much in the name of Christ. Like the woman who thought she'd read to some sick and needy kids and wound up with a warehouse full of children's books. And the man and his wife who'd lost a daughter but gained the children from so many families in a Christmas celebration they'll remember forever. And the chiropractor who found perspective by going to the homeless in the inner city.

I imagined the looks on the faces of the hundreds of thousands of people who will learn about Jesus this year as a result of a single $100 bill.

Not only has the original $10,000 increased to more than $150,000, but those hundred people laid the groundwork to *directly* impact nearly 250,000 locally, nationally, and internationally with their Kingdom building efforts. We are convinced this is just the beginning.

God has begun something in this little experiment that needs the attention of the whole Christian community. You see, it is required of stewards, says the apostle Paul, that they "must prove faithful" (1 Corinthians 4:2). And the question is, will God find *us* faithful to the call?

Another interesting question that arose from the Kingdom Assignment was this: Who benefited most from the project—those who were served or those who did the serving? Leesa and four others interviewed nearly every one of the hundred participants and recorded their comments. What they said will not soon be forgotten.

In one way or another, they all said this: *"We were the ones who benefited most from participating in the Kingdom Assignment."* And they were right. As much as they thought and prayed and worked to make the most of their $100, they were still the ones who benefited most from the whole experience because of the lessons they learned along the way.

The Top Six Things They Told Us . . .

1. *"We received more than we ever gave."*

If we heard this once, we heard it a hundred times. Literally. Over and over again from everyone we interviewed. For some, like Vicki, it was the blessing of seeing her investment at work. She used her $100 to buy four mud troughs that will be used over and over again to build houses for the poor in Mexico.

"I knew I wanted to use the money in a way that would help people for years to come," she said. Vicki actually boarded a church bus and traveled across the border, where she rolled up her sleeves and helped build such a house. When the day was over, she exclaimed, "When I literally saw how the money was working, I was overwhelmed with emotion."

For Mike, the blessing was the thrill of becoming someone important to a child. Mike, remember, invested his $100 in a program for abused children. More important, after years of being beaten and abused as a child, years of needing help from others, the Kingdom Assignment allowed Mike to help someone else—a boy as lonely and hurt as he had once been.

"Maybe," he told me, "just maybe I'll be there for a child who was ready to end it all. A child like me."

2. "God answers prayer."

As a pastor I'm supposed to say, "God answers prayer," and even speak about it. But the fact is, many of us, pastors included, often wonder at times if our prayers are really being heard, let alone answered. Take the time when a single young mother in our congregation died of cancer leaving four young children behind. Susan had suffered for years. We wanted more than anything to see her healed, but that didn't happen.

And yet the people who participated in the Kingdom Assignment recognized firsthand that when you set out to accomplish something for God, prayers get answered in a variety of different ways, some of which can't be explained.

Most of these people had no idea what they were going to do with this money when they first received their marching orders. Would they hand it over to a street person? Give it to their favorite charity? Use it to buy socks for a men's shelter?

In fact, I'm sure they would have found it easier if I'd handed out specific instructions about what to do with the $100. But this wasn't about doing what the pastor wanted or the church wanted them to do. This was about doing what the Master wanted them to do. In other words, they needed to spend some time thinking and seeking and praying about what that would entail.

Some felt their hearts racing within them, some felt their faces grow hot with anger, others returned to their seats biting their nails, completely in the dark about how to invest $100 in God's Kingdom. Some felt sick to their stomachs from the weight of the responsibility.

But in the end, God came through with flying colors for each of them.

Renee said, "I've learned not to panic when God calls anymore. Instead, I choose to have faith and believe that God will provide. God answers prayer, I know that now, and He can do more than we can imagine with $100 and a willing servant."

More indeed.

In Renee's case, the $100 was used to touch the lives of 150 elderly shut-in residents of a local convalescent hospital. She used her money to buy materials, and then invited children in her neighborhood to spend a Saturday morning in her garage making personal Christmas cards for the patients. When the holiday rolled around, they delivered the gift cards to each one personally.

Steven would echo the same lesson. A freshman in high school, there are a lot of things Steven hasn't seen growing up in the affluence of South Orange County. Like poverty. What does a fourteen-year-old do when he's given $100 and told to use it to glorify God and benefit others? "I prayed," Steven said, "and God showed me what to do with it."

He heard about a family in the area who couldn't afford to buy a table for their meals. As a result, this family ate all their meals together off the floor of their small apartment. Steven was moved to buy them a dining room table to fulfill his assignment. They were shocked and overjoyed. A fourteen-year-old boy learned a lesson we can all afford to learn. No matter how small the amount, the gift of giving brings greater joy than the gift itself.

3. "It all belongs to God."

I think this was the lesson I was hoping to teach and praying people would catch as a result of my sermon. But a sermon can't change us like a life lesson can. You see, I don't think this assignment was really about the money. Rather it was about the participants' attitudes toward money.

One man said, "I asked myself why I felt so differently about this $100 than other money in my wallet or bank account. The answer was clear: God wanted me to think of everything I had as coming from Him. It no longer belonged to me."

The man was right. It comes down to the role we take on—whether as steward or owner.

One of my favorite stories from the Kingdom Assignment period was told by a volunteer who decided not to spend his specific $100 bill, but instead, to keep it in his wallet as a constant reminder that "all his money," and "all his possessions," and "all his assets," and "all his treasures" really belong to God. Every now and then God will put a person or a cause in this man's way that requires him to give away the $100.

And every time, he finds a crisp new $100 bill and places it back in his wallet.

4. *"A little can go a long way."*

I have often wondered what it must have been like to be in the crowd on a day when Jesus did a miracle. "How would I have responded?" I ask myself. Take the feeding of the five thousand, for instance. I have stood on the hillsides along the Sea of Galilee and overlooked the sites where the multiplying of the loaves and fishes likely took place. It's rather remarkable to let your imagination go and think of what it must have really been like to witness that event in the first century. But again, how would I have responded?

From the meager resources of a young boy's simple lunch and response to Jesus, a whole community was fed. Nothing short of a kind of miracle of multiplication took place again in the lives of these hundred people. Quite clearly, God did for the participants of the Kingdom Assignment the very thing He did that day in Galilee.

He multiplied it, miraculously and in His power.

Craig the chiropractor has realized that. After making the initial Kingdom investment for burgers for the homeless on skid row in L.A, he gives away that much each month to help ease the pain of others. "It amazed me," he said, "to understand how a little investment in time and money could have such a profound impact on others and myself." Amazing indeed!

Another participant agreed it would be fascinating to see what would happen if all our earthly belongings—including our bodies and minds—were considered God's property. "It's truly something what might be accomplished if we looked at all our finances from the following perspective: 'How would God have me use these resources to make an eternal difference for His Kingdom?'"

"The key," he said, "is looking at everything from a Kingdom perspective."

5. *"Opportunities are all around us every day."*

When Janet and Don's friends lost a child, they wondered if there was anything they could do to help them through this time of grief. When they accepted the Kingdom Assignment, they decided to use their $100 to create gift packs for couples in hospitals who have just lost a baby or small child. While they were pursuing this idea, Janet became pregnant and was a little concerned her new excitement would be a deterrent in her desire to comfort others. Unfortunately, a few short weeks later Janet miscarried. Her newfound perspective on grief was the catalyst that will keep this program going for years to come. She now could relate firsthand and felt it was an important piece to her life's journey in being able to relate with others.

"The feeling of handing over one of our packets to a devastated mom and dad is something I'll never forget," Janet said afterward, "as though all our pain, tears, and grief suddenly had meaning."

As the ministry of the gift packets grew, Janet and Don felt an infusion of hope in their hearts, something that has pulled them from the dark places of defeat over the miscarriage they experienced. "Suddenly I could see everything through God's eyes," Janet said. "I could look at every situation, feel every situation through the eyes and heart of God."

A new pair of eyes and a new heart—that's what this is all about. Having eyes to see what we often look past without a thought. Having a heart tender to the call of God and His people.

Doug called it the need in his life to "be more willing to put myself in *uncharted territory.*" What a great way to identify it. Uncharted territory. Each of us is often so busy and preoccupied with our own-chartered agendas that we can easily miss the opportunity God presents to make a difference in someone's life. A kind word, a simple gesture, an investment of time, attention, compassion, generosity. The opportunities are all around us every day. We live and work in a world of people who need to see that God cares and makes a difference. You and I may be the only glimpse of Jesus some people will ever see.

Another thing the Kingdom Assignment did was help people be bold in their faith. Sometimes we Christians think of witnessing for Christ as something we do totally apart from anything else. We step out of our normal lives and go into a carefully prepared monologue on the plan of salvation.

And we wonder why people think we're strange, or worse, why they don't respond.

Witnessing for Christ isn't some obligation set apart as "time to talk about God." Rather, it's something we do every day of our lives. It's who we are and where we go, what we do, as well as what we say. All of our thoughts, actions, and words are a living billboard for Jesus and His Kingdom.

Take Michael, for example. After a life of living in the limelight athletically, most of his friends had no idea he was a believer. But when it came to carrying out the Kingdom Assignment, talking about his faith became merely a way of explaining his heart's desire.

You see, I don't think people want to hear a sermon. They want to see one lived out in the lives of the believers around them. Authenticity will always have an audience. It always has, and always will. The question becomes this: Is the faith we profess *real* in our own lives?

6. *"I discovered what's really important."*

This was the fun part—the truths people learned that shook them to the core, things they had never expected.

For instance, here is the greatest lesson Craig learned from his time giving back adjustments and hamburgers to people on skid row: "I had one guy come up to me during my first visit there and tell me that he thanked God every morning for being able to see the sun rise."

Craig could barely tell me that story without getting tears in his eyes. "Up to that day I was very stressed about things in life, like finances, work, family. It took the vision of a homeless man to bring me out of my self-pity and into a life where I appreciate what God has done for me."

There is nothing like a dose of reality to wake us up to what's really important, is there? And sometimes those moments come to us from unlikely sources: a child asking us whether we have money for the Salvation Army man at Christmastime, the grateful words of an amputee more thankful for life than discouraged about the loss of a limb, the eighty-year-old woman arriving at church an hour early for extra time to reflect.

Hmm.

Is there really anything more important in life than one day hearing God say to you personally, "Well done, good and faithful servant"? I don't think so. One day all the things we think are so important here on earth will be gone, and all that will remain is Jesus' words. The only matter of importance will be whether we loved and honored God and His people with our beings and belongings. Jesus said, "Seek first the kingdom of God and his righteousness," and everything else you need to really live in this world will be added unto you.

That's a lesson worth learning, a reward worth living and reaching for.

The Kingdom Is in Us

You see, I believe God wants His Kingdom to grow, both in us and through us. It's like the mustard seed, which starts out smaller than all the other plants. But add a little water and sunshine and that seed becomes one of the biggest plants of all.

So it is with the Kingdom Assignment.

A little investment mixed with love, faith, and obedience can go a long way—in fact, beyond your wildest imagination. That was brought to my attention again after the Kingdom Assignment began and other people wanted to join in using their own funds.

Several couples attended an informal dinner hosted by one of our pastors to present an opportunity in China. The pitch went out from a guest speaker of the Underground Church, a church that has grown from 85,000 people fifty years ago to over 85,000,000 today despite the oppression of the communist Chinese government. "Help us," the man told the group of self-appointed Kingdom Assignment participants. "We need a place to train pastors in China."

Apparently nothing like this had ever been built in China. That night among those Kingdom-minded couples, there was one husband and wife who felt God prompting them to write a check for the entire amount of $50,000 needed for the training facility.

"In some ways it was as though the Kingdom was being built before our eyes," one woman said about the evening. "One dollar at a time, one willing heart at a time. The Kingdom was within us all along."

I believe we have yet to see the array of great things God wants to do in and through His church if and when His people begin to think and live like faithful people.

CHAPTER 6

Like Wildfire

If you have ever visited or lived in Southern California in autumn, you know we don't get much change in our weather. No, instead we're stuck with the same boring eighty degrees day in, day out.

But autumn in Southern California does have one major drawback. Autumn is fire season. It happens every September, October, and November. The gentle winds shift from the standard off-shore afternoon breezes to the warm, whipped up Santa Ana desert winds. And every time they do, a high alert goes out for wildfires.

You may have seen some of our famous, or infamous, autumn fires on the evening news. Each year, hundreds of thousands of acres are burned, homes are lost, and lives are threatened by fires that often get started with a simple "spark."

The Power in a Single Spark

We witnessed this personally in the fall of 1982. Leesa and I had been invited by our friend Bob Field, who at that time was the defensive coordinator for the UCLA football team, to be his guest at the annual UCLA/USC football game at the Rose Bowl in Pasadena. If you're a diehard Bruin fan, as we are, you can understand the magnitude of this annual rivalry and the excitement of having the opportunity to witness it with our own eyes. So we jumped at the chance.

We had heard on the news that morning of a small fire that had started in the hills, but we didn't think much of it. We figured the fire department would have it out in no time. Around noon we left our two young daughters with friends in nearby Agoura Hills and headed for a day of great college football action and rivalry in Pasadena, some forty miles away. It was a great game. UCLA won and we rejoiced.

Until, that is, we got news of the unexpected and rapid growth of the fire back at home.

I will never forget the feeling I had as we drove back into the Conejo Valley in the early evening and saw, as far as the eye could see, the charred remains of what were, even that morning, beautiful, green flowing hills. It happened so fast the firefighters didn't have a chance to stop it. The sixty-mile-per-hour winds had whipped the flames into a frenzy that threatened homes and entire neighborhoods. The family baby-sitting our girls was among those already evacuated.

In an unstoppable drive west, the flames literally jumped eight full-size lanes of massive freeway in an instant, and left a charred and flattened path twenty miles through Malibu Canyon and down to the beach. It was frightening and awesome. We were stunned.

That day an unforgettable impression was left in our minds of how one spark can make an immediate difference in our world.

A Different Kind of Fire

It would be nearly twenty years later, on another autumn day, that I would see a day that marked a spark that launched a fire of a different kind. A fire that would not destroy but rather rapidly grow the Kingdom of God.

A week after the Kingdom Assignment was handed out, word reached a reporter at our local newspaper, the *Aliso Viejo News*. When this reporter heard the story about the church that gave $100 to a hundred people, she felt it was a story worth telling. She wrote an article and titled it, "Church Pays It Forward."

Overnight we were being contacted by the *Orange County Register*, then by the Associated Press, which wanted to run the article on the national newswire. In just a few weeks from the day the project was started, the story of the Kingdom Assignment hit the front pages of more than 10,000 newspapers across the United States, including the *Washington Post*, the *Boston Globe*, the *Seattle Times*, and the *Chicago Tribune*.

The simple story was sweeping the country like wildfire.

There were radio interviews and calls from NBC's *Dateline*, asking if they could follow several participants with cameras to capture the results of their investment. *People* magazine and *Woman's Day* magazine began telling the stories of faith.

And what was happening in the process?

The money we'd invested in God's Kingdom was being used not only to multiply His work but also to glorify God. Time and again the participants would tell a reporter, "This isn't about me, it's about God. It's His money, His assignment."

Wendell was new to our church, but he was paying attention. After watching and listening to the course of events surrounding the one hundred participants in the Kingdom Assignment, he decided he didn't want to be left simply watching from the sidelines. So he did something about it.

Wendell owns an aftermarket motorcycle parts and accessories company. For years he used to race motorcycles professionally. Now, he makes them look good. It's one of the largest companies of its kind in the country, and he employs seventy people. One day in light of the Kingdom Assignment, he initiated a plan he knew would stun his staff.

He called a mandatory meeting of his entire staff. Since there was some secrecy about the nature of this meeting, many of the people thought they were going to receive bad news or worse, lose their jobs.

Instead, they each received a crisp new $100 bill. All seventy-seven of them! Wendell told them the story of our church's initial example and the reasons why we did what we did. Then he divided them into teams that crossed employment levels and assigned them the task of using their combined resources to help the community.

When the shock wore off, they were ecstatic and began thinking of a number of ways to bless people! Who would do such a thing? I'll tell you. Someone with a mind to see his own Kingdom Assignment grow and multiply to impact the lives of others and glorify the name and purpose of our great God.

By the end of November, more and more among the recipients and participants in the Kingdom Assignment were beginning to identify the focus of their best efforts in an attempt to glorify God and benefit others. There were all kinds of different ideas, but each idea was prayerfully considered in order to help grow God's Kingdom values in some unique, if not creative way.

Greg was sitting near the back of the church when I announced the Kingdom Assignment. He told me later that he really didn't want to be there that night. In fact, he wanted to be just about anywhere but in church. Several years back, he and his wife and family had gotten involved in helping launch a new church. In fact, Greg served on the first elder board of the new work.

Things weren't easy, as is often the case in new ministries, but through a set of rather negative circumstances and a devastating moral failure on the part of one of the church leaders, the young church had closed its doors, disillusioning many, including Greg. He later would confess to me that never again was he going to put himself in such a vulnerable position with any church, nor with God.

As I walked down the middle aisle that day looking for volunteers for the Kingdom Assignment, Greg's face caught my eye. In the absence of people stepping forward in that service, I volunteered Greg. He was stuck. While everything in him wanted to escape, reluctantly, he made his way to the front of the church to receive his assignment.

Little did Greg know it would set off a spark and kick-start his heart for the Lord and for ministry. Greg became actively involved in the church again. He moved from the back row to the second row. The numbing hurt from the past just melted away. No one was happier than his wife, who was thrilled to see in Greg the God-given talents that she had always admired in him.

People in the Fire's Path

Shortly after the Associated Press article came out, we received a letter from a prisoner. Charles was an articulate man who had made quite a few mistakes in his life and he was paying the price. He had read the story in his local paper in northern California. In the letter he spoke about his life and why he was in jail. Drug abuse had led him to make several bad choices. He didn't make excuses and he wasn't asking for anything for himself but was in great turmoil over his family. He knew he had left his wife and two sons unprotected and felt sad that he was not there to be the husband and father he should be.

Leesa's heart was touched by the man's plight. She prayed and believed God had a purpose in allowing us to know Charles.

Within a month of receiving his letter, Leesa contacted Charles's wife for the first time. Although she was hesitant to believe in the kindness of strangers, she has since allowed us to help her earn a driver's license. Not long ago we were even able to give her a car through our church's car ministry.

Many prayers, letters, and phone calls have been exchanged since then. Men from our church have befriended Charles and are in constant contact. When he gets out of prison in a few months, we plan to help him with housing, a job, and the chance to start life over. The news article was the spark that became a wildfire in Charles's heart and gave him hope.

You never know where that spark will ignite a flame that will take someone into eternity. And many sparks will become flames we won't know about until we reach eternity.

Won't it be an amazing sight to see?

CHAPTER 7

Accepting Your Own Kingdom Assignment

At the beginning of this book I told you I had an assignment for you, and this is it: God is calling you to experience something you've probably only dreamed of—a leading role in the building of His eternal Kingdom.

Are you excited? You should be. There are no limits to what God will do if you are willing to accept the assignment.

The best part is that it doesn't matter if you're busy, untrained, or ill-equipped. That was the case for everyone who participated in the Kingdom Assignment, and look at what was accomplished. We have power, so much untapped power.

Push-ups for God

Leesa heard a story the other day that was scary but inspiring.

A man was enjoying an evening with his wife at a worship service at his home church. He heard the Lord say something to him loud and clear.

Get into the aisle and do ten push-ups, God said.

The man looked around to see if anyone else had heard the voice, but people were carrying on as before. *Must be my imagination,* he thought. Then the command came again.

Get into the aisle and do ten push-ups.

Right here, Lord, right now? You can't mean it. I'm going to humiliate myself and embarrass my wife.

Get into the aisle and do—

Fine. He stepped into the middle aisle with gusto, did ten push-ups, and returned to his seat. His wife stared at him, a look of horror on her face. He shrugged his shoulders and decided he would tell her later, even though he wasn't too sure she would believe him.

When the service was over, a man, assisted by his wife, came up to the man who had done the push-ups. This man, who seemed strong and confident, was crying and tried to make sense through his tears.

"I . . . I was sitting in the back of the church and . . . I really didn't want to be here tonight." He wiped the tears from his face. "I was bitter and frustrated with

God . . . I wanted some form of proof that there even was a God."

His weeping continued. "I decided to test Him." He swallowed hard, struggling to find his voice. "I told God . . . the only way I would believe in Him was if someone in the congregation would spontaneously do ten push-ups in the middle aisle."

Whoa! Do you have the chills yet? That man prayed with his new friend to receive Christ, and neither one of them will ever be the same.

What will God call on you to do? Maybe a handstand on your next trip to the grocery store?

Listen for His Assignment Orders

I know that since the Kingdom Assignment began, I listen much more closely to God. I take every opportunity I can to give money away. It doesn't take much. The other day I went to our local drug store and saw Girl Scouts out front selling cookies. I had just finished off the third box of Thin Mints (the best cookie in the world), and I was not interested in being tempted by more of the same. I smiled when I walked in and felt a feeling of dread knowing I was going to be confronted as I left the store with the cute, smiling faces of Girl Scouts.

As I left the store I did something I will never forget, something I plan to repeat many times in the days ahead. The Girl Scouts rushed toward me with boxes in hand, and I simply smiled and handed them five dollars. "Thanks," I told them, "but you can keep the cookies."

They squealed with excitement, as if I had just handed them, well, a hundred dollars.

What's your assignment? We all have them. Jeremiah wrote, "'For I know the plans I have for you,' says the LORD, 'plans to prosper you and . . . to give you hope and a future'" (Jeremiah 29:11).

There are lifetime assignments and daily assignments.

We recently heard Bill Hybels, senior pastor of Willow Creek Community Church in South Barrington, Illinois, speak at a conference. He talked about missing an opportunity at a local hardware store. He watched as a woman struggled to get a load of wood into her car, but Bill was tired and had a lot on his mind, so he walked right by her, climbed in his car, and headed home. He really didn't think much about the missed opportunity to help until later that evening. His point was this: We call on God to get us involved in His Kingdom, but many times He has given us everything we need to get in the game. We are God's tools and His instruments. We'll have the power and resources to truly be His Kingdom builders in all situations if we just have eyes to see.

Even when we're tired, untrained, or ill-equipped.

I have a friend who is a marriage and family therapist. She has a patient struggling with depression with whom she has met on a regular basis for quite some time.

One day the woman she was treating bounded into her weekly session with an unrecognizable smile on her face.

"What's up?" my friend asked her.

The patient sat down, her back straight, her limbs trembling from excitement. "God used me this week, and it's changed my life."

She proceeded to tell a story I will call the "cold meat story." Earlier that week as she was standing in line at her neighborhood grocery store, she watched a woman staring at the items on the conveyer belt. "It was clear she was trying to think about what to put back," the patient explained. "I knew in my heart she was having money problems."

Finally, the stranger took out a package of cold meat and handed it back to the cashier. Then she paid her bill and left.

"In that moment I could hear God telling me to buy the meat." The patient smiled. "I argued with Him for about a minute. After all, the woman was gone and I figured I'd never catch her. But God's words in my heart were insistent. 'Buy the meat!'"

Once she got to the register, she waited until the cashier was done with her order and then sheepishly asked if she could buy the cold meat sitting on the side of the cash register. The cashier lowered her brow. "You sure you don't want some fresh meat?"

"No," the patient said. "I want that meat."

As she carried her own groceries and the small package of cold meat into the parking lot, she doubted whether God had really asked her to buy it. After all, the poor stranger was probably gone. As she crossed the lane in front of the store the patient was nearly run over by a car driven by. . .

That's right, the poor stranger.

The patient took the package of meat, went to the stranger's car window, and handed it to her. They both began to cry as the patient told the poor stranger, "God told me to buy this for you."

A Few Things to Consider

What's involved in accepting a Kingdom Assignment of your own? Bottom line: there are a few things to consider or reconsider.

First is a decision on your part to know who Jesus is in your life.

Is Jesus your King?

The answer to that one question has huge implications. We Americans don't particularly value kings. Have you noticed that? We fought a war two hundred years ago with England to rid ourselves of the sovereignty of a king. We value independence, autonomy, freedom. Even freedom to make wrong choices.

The Bible, however, values the sovereignty of God, the rule of God, the reign of God, dependence on God, which frees us to become all we were truly meant to be—children of God, heirs of His promises, subjects of His Kingdom.

Let me ask you again, Is Jesus your King? You see, the values of His Kingdom won't be considered valuable if we think of Him as anything less than whom the Bible rightly declares Him in fact to be.

Second, accepting your Kingdom Assignment will involve consciously transferring the title on everything you consider yours so that it now becomes His. It's a subtle shift, but a profound one. No longer is it "my" house or "my" car or "my" money or "my" stuff, but now, in my heart, it all belongs to Him. The question is: "What am I going to do each and every day with the resources and gifts and talents and assets that my King has entrusted to me?"

Third, accepting your Kingdom Assignment will involve seeking God's direction through prayer. Today, we often consider "seekers" as only those who have yet to discover a relationship with God. Believers, we think, are "finders." But the Scriptures portray believers as lifetime seekers. And one of the prayers we can all begin to whisper is "I'm ready and waiting, God. Show me my assignment."

As the Kingdom Assignment grew, our children's department gave $25 to a handful of children anxious to take part in the project. The results proved the only thing God needs is a willing heart. Here are some of the results that came from the children among us.

- *Lauren, third grade:* Lauren wrote a letter to family members, asking them to join her. She raised more than $400 and bought puppets for a Vacation Bible School in Spain this summer.

- *Kyler, third grade:* Kyler bought devotional books for all the boys in his class at school. He wrote a letter to each of them, telling them about how much he loves Jesus, and that he wanted them to love Him too. His mom was a bit worried about doing this at a public school, but she spoke with the principal, who approved it.

- *McKena, fourth grade:* McKena invested in her local home school program that was struggling with finances.

- *Collin, second grade:* After going on a mission trip to Mexico, Collin knew the needs of the people there. He wrote out a speech on a note card and presented his assignment to two hundred men at a Bible study, asking them to join him in giving. After he gave his talk he ran out to the parking lot, hugged his mom, and said, "The Holy Spirit gave me the courage!" That day $539 was raised to purchase food, blankets, and building materials for the Mexican people.

- *Cory, third grade:* Cory sent twenty-five letters to family and friends asking them to match his $25. He collected approximately $500 and donated it to a new after-school program for troubled teens.

- *Joel, fifth grade:* Joel bought toiletries, collected clothing, and needed items, and took these things to Laura's House, a shelter for abused and battered women and children.

- *Hayden Arnold, second grade:* Hayden's little friend, Karina, had a cancerous brain tumor removed recently. He took Karina out for ice cream and gave her the rest of the money, hoping it will help her pay for surgery.

- *Heather, fifth grade:* She gave her money to Orangewood Children's Home, a place for abused children.

- *Jordan, fourth grade:* Jordan bought a friend a Bible and brought her to church.

- *Chloe, fourth grade:* Chloe bought food, collected old clothes from her closet, and sent them with her grandmother on a mission trip to Mexico.

The Bible says, "And a little child will lead them" (Isaiah 11:6). That has certainly been the case with the Kingdom Assignment.

Maybe you are saying, "I could never do this. I don't have the time or energy or resources. I wouldn't know where to start."

For you I say, simply pray. Pray daily about your assignment and remember there are no limits to God's checkbook. Ask others to pray as to how God will make this happen. He is faithful. If we humble ourselves before the Lord, He is faithful and just to answer those prayers. God can do anything, even move the hand of an elder or deacon board. If you want a changed heart, a changed life . . . if you want to make a lasting difference in the Kingdom while there's still time, nothing will stop you.

Absolutely nothing.

Do you realize what would happen if every believer would take on such a Kingdom Assignment? Do you realize what would happen if *you* would decide to take this assignment on? The dreaming and praying begins today.

Your assignment is just around the corner.

Let the spark ignite and watch the wildfire begin!

♛

We want to hear from you. Please send your comments about this book to us in care of the address below. Thank you.

GRAND RAPIDS, MICHIGAN 49530

www.zondervan.com

👑

Has this book encouraged you to accomplish your own Kingdom Assignment? If so, we want to hear about it. Please log on to **www.kingdomassignment.com** and tell us your story and/or be inspired by others who have taken on a Kingdom challenge that God has put on their heart.